Varsha's Varanasi

Second reprint May 2023

Text: Chitra Soundar
Photography and Design: Soumitra Ranade
Featuring: Mayanka and Raja

Karadi Tales Company Pvt. Ltd.
3A Dev Regency, 11 First Main Road,
Gandhinagar, Adyar, Chennai 600020
Tel.: +91-44-42054243
email: contact@karaditales.com
www.karaditales.com

ISBN: 978-81-8190-348-8

VARSHA'S

Varanasi

Written by

Chitra Soundar

Photography and Design

Soumitra Ranade

Featuring

Mayanka and Raja

"Varsha! Papa has forgotten his spectacles," called out Ma.

Varsha's father, Shambhu, was a tour guide in the sacred city of Varanasi. Varsha knew his route well.

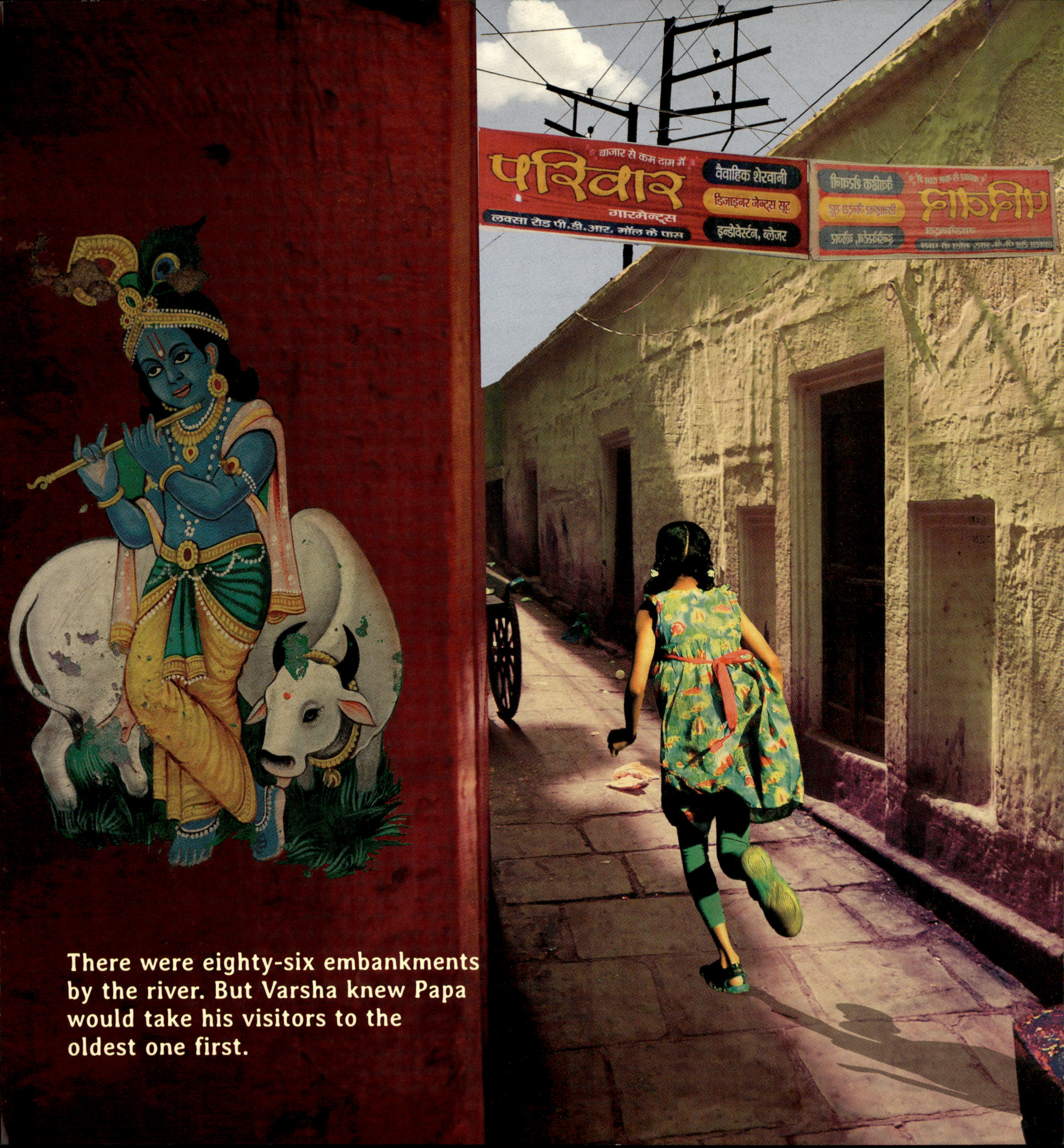

There were eighty-six embankments by the river. But Varsha knew Papa would take his visitors to the oldest one first.

CK34/36

She looked around the ghat. Pilgrims were bathing in the river, tourists were taking photos. But Papa was not with them.

"Don't hurry in Varanasi," called out a shopkeeper.

“Shambhu went to the temple,” shouted Bhairav Kaka, the paan-seller.

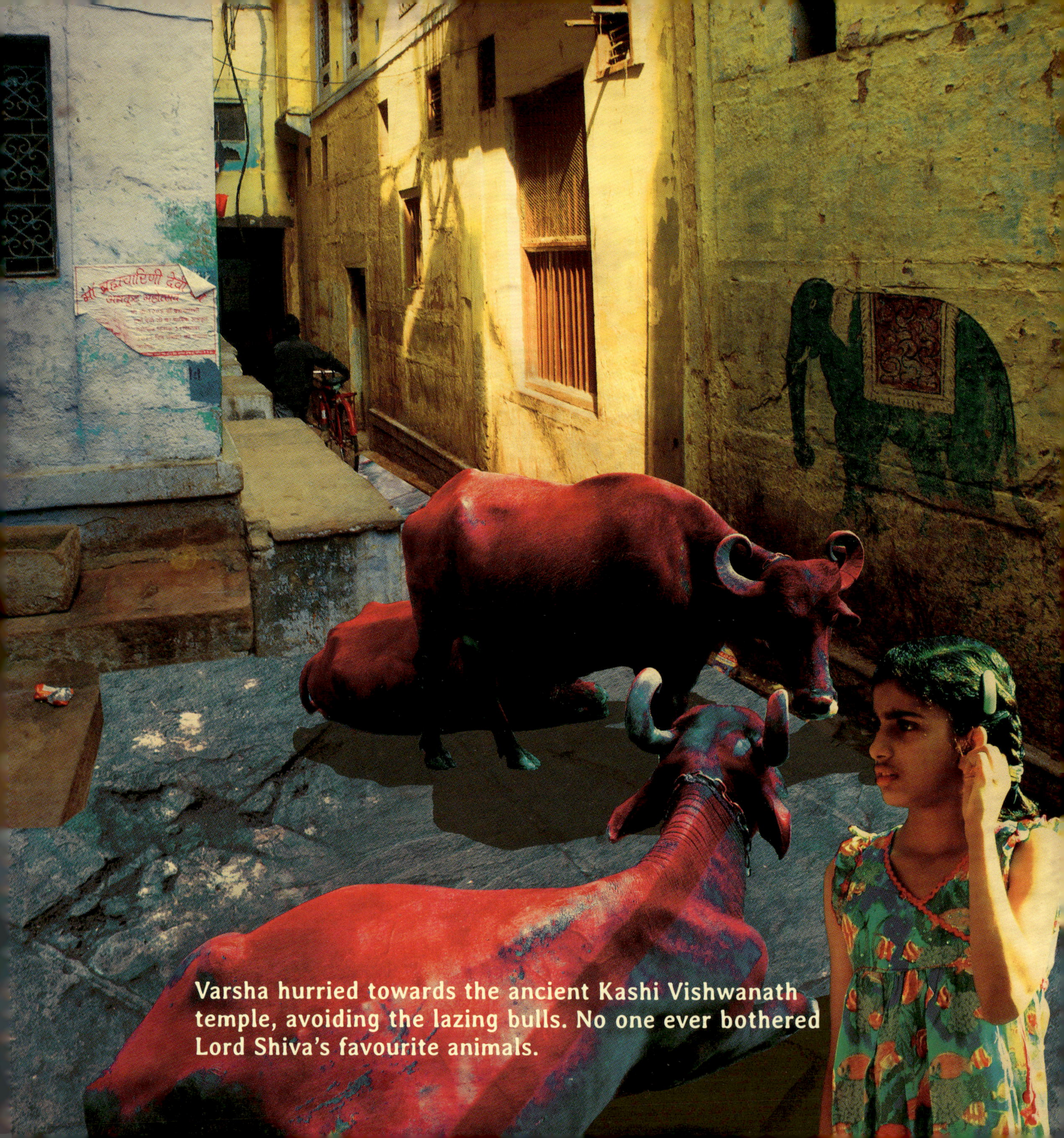

Varsha hurried towards the ancient Kashi Vishwanath temple, avoiding the lazing bulls. No one ever bothered Lord Shiva's favourite animals.

नेपाली धर्मशाला
माँ ब्रह्मचारिणी
अन्नकूट
श्री श्री 1008 मां
दुर्गा देवी जी का
2014 दिन
जायेगा।

The temple was crowded. People came from all over India and spoke many different languages.

Varsha hoped they weren't saying bad things about the river Ganga. She looked for her Papa's orange umbrella. No sign of it.

"Shambhu went to Manikarnika,"
said the sadhu outside the temple.

मानसरोवर
मणिक
र्णिका
घाट
MANIK
ARNIKA

Tourists often wanted to see the open cremations at Manikarnika ghat.
But that didn't interest Varsha. Whenever she went there,
she looked for Lord Shiva's earring on the steps instead.

Her grandmother said that it fell off there when Shiva was dancing.
Would it turn up like a fossil?

No orange umbrella, no Papa.
Where could he be?

Usually the next stop would be the Kal Bhairava temple. Kal Bhairava was the policeman of Varanasi and pilgrims went there to pay their respects.

TRING! TRING!

"Looking for your Papa?"
asked Rafiq.
"Come, let's check the temple."
TreeBaba
HANDMADE
RECYCLED
COTTON PAPER

Rafiq took Papa's visitors to temples and shops. He knew interesting things about Varanasi that couldn't be found in books.

The temple was noisy and it smelt of camphor. Many waited to buy bracelets to ward off evil eyes.

But Papa wasn't there either.

"Next stop - Alamgiri Mosque," said Varsha.

The mosque was on their way back home anyway.

"This mosque was built by Aurangzeb," said Rafiq. "His father built the Taj Mahal."

Varsha smiled. "You have told me that before."

It was prayer time at the mosque. There were no tourists.

"Maybe he took the tourists to the silk sari shop," said Rafiq.

Inside the shop, many silk saris in rainbow colours were on display. The shop was busy.

But Papa was not there.

"Check the terrace," said the shop manager. "Tourists go up there to see the city."

Varanasi looked different
from the terrace.

The river was like a long silk
sari spread out over the city.

Boats drifted slowly.

"He isn't here," said Rafiq.
"I'll drop you home."

On their way, the smell of kachoris floated past. Papa often advised his tourists never to refuse one when offered.

"I've been looking for you everywhere."

"Your glasses," said Varsha, putting her hand in her pocket to pull them out. But what was this?

There was a big gaping hole in her pocket!

“PAPA!” she called out.

As they turned a corner... was that Papa? Varsha jumped off the rickshaw and darted through the crowded alleys.

"Don't worry, beta," said Papa. "I would know Varanasi even with my eyes closed. Anyway, it was time to change that old pair."

That night, Varsha went with Papa to watch the evening arathi.

"Tell me the stories of the ghats, Papa," said Varsha.

Though she had heard the stories of the ghats many times before, Varsha loved to hear them again and again.

As tourists made their way back,
Papa and Varsha sat down at the ghats
and watched the river and the skies above.

CISF Complex
Varanasi
GT Rd
HARI NAGAR COLONY
Chhittupur Rd
LAHARTARA
SHIVPURWA
IP Mall Sigra
MATAKUND
SHASTRI NAGAR
LALLAPURA
GOLGHAR
NEW LOCO COLONY
Sonia Rd
DLW Rd
Overhead Water Tank
CHHITTUPURA
Purana Pan Daba
Sigra-Siddhigiri Bagh Rd
JAI PRAKASH NAGAR
SIGRA
JAHUMANDI
GODAULIA
LUXA
Luxa Rd
NIRALA NAGAR
Sigra - Mahmoorganj Rd
Rathyatra - Mahmoorganj Rd
Mahmoorganj Rd
LIC St
Raja Moti Chand Rd
BHELUPUR
ASHFAQ NAGAR
GIRI NAGAR COLONY
SRI NAGAR
GURUBAGH
KAMCHCHHA
Kamachha Rd
74
VINAYAKA KOLHWA
Manduadih
TULSIPUR
Jal Kal
RAILWAY COLONY
BAZARDIHA
SUDAMAPUR
IP Vijaya Mall
Wyndham Fall
Peace Point Rd
Kirahiya Rd
SRI RAM NAGAR COLONY
KHOJWAN
KIRAHIYA
JAWAHAR NAGAR COLONY
SARAI NANDAN
NAWABGANJ
JJANKI NAGAR
TRIDEV NAGAR COLONY
Badi Patiya Rd
Kabir Nagar Rd
NAGWA
TULSI NAGAR
NEW COLONY KAKARMATTA
SUNDARPUR

As they sat on the edge of the ghat, Varsha noticed a pair of glasses floating towards them.

Papa's glasses!

The Dashashwamedh ghat, where the Ganga arathi happened, had been her first stop while looking for Papa.

Map of Varanasi

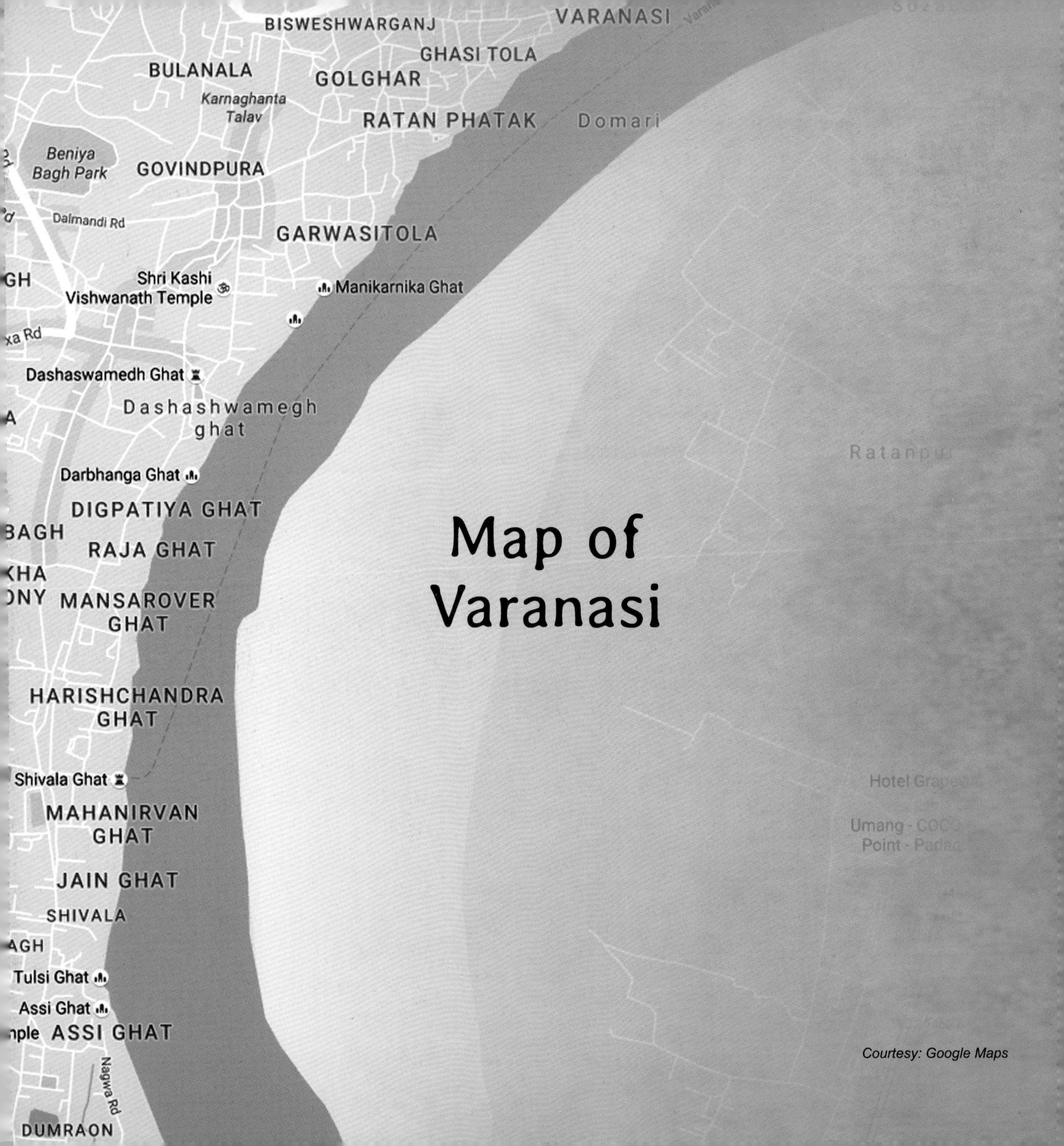

Courtesy: Google Maps

About Varanasi

The name Varanasi comes from the names of the two rivers that flow through it - Varuna and Assi. Many Hindus believe they will be released from the cycle of rebirth if they die in Varanasi, and choose to spend their last days there.

Like its most popular resident, Lord Shiva, the city has many names. Also referred to as Kashi and Benares, it is one of the oldest cities in India. The river Ganga is at the centre of this city's ancient history, its modern trade, and its connection to the rest of India.

Archaeological evidence suggests that the city has been inhabited since the 11th century BCE. It has been a centre for music, art, crafts, and trade ever since.

A place of worship is never complete without festivals and Varanasi's most important one is the Maha Shivarathri festival where Hindus fast all night in honour of Lord Shiva. Diwali, the festival of lights is also a visual feast as visitors can see thousands of lamps lit up and floating on the river.

Varanasi has historical importance for other religions as well. It was only ten kilometres away from the city where Buddha gave his first sermon. Moreover, the city is dotted by mosques built by Aurangzeb and Akbar.

The city is a traveller's delight. Whether it is buying Benares silk saris, taking pictures with monkeys in the temples, or frequenting roadside kachori and betelnut leaf shops, there's something for everyone.

Facts about Varanasi

Varanasi
A chaotic and colourful city, Varanasi's streets are thronged by thousands of tourists every day for its religious, historical and cultural significance. As a result, it is known as the city that never sleeps.
The city's economy is fuelled by small-scale industries and household production. Some of India's finest artisans are found on the streets of the city.

Embankments by the river
Varanasi's most striking oddities are ghats, or embankments made in stone that lead to the river Ganga. The ghats in Varanasi are famous around the world. It is a widespread belief in India that a holy bath in the Ganges can free one of their sins. Hence, it is a common sight to see pilgrims perform rituals on a ghat and take a dip in the Ganges. Some ghats are also exclusively used as Hindu cremation sites.

Dashashwamedh Ghat
In Sanskrit, dash means ten; ashwa, horse; and medh, sacrifice. The Dashashwamedh Ghat, located close to the Kashi Vishwanath Temple, is said to be the oldest and the most spectacular of the ghats in Varanasi. It is believed that Lord Brahma sacrificed ten horses here during the Dashashwamedh Yajna performed in the ghat and thus, the name. Every evening, the Ganga arathi is performed on this ghat.

Ganga
River Ganga is the life force of India. It flows from the Gangotri, in southern Himalayas to the Bay of Bengal, running 2525 km long. The Ganga basin covers 26% of the country. The Ganga is personified as a goddess in Hindu mythology. She is well-known as a consort of Lord Shiva. Ganga is called Tripathaga in Sanskrit meaning the one who travels the three worlds (heaven, earth and hell). Today the major concern is to save the sacred river from pollution.

The Kachori Gali
Extremely popular in South Asia, kachoris are fried and flattened circular breads that are stuffed with moong dal and a mixture of spices. Near the Kashi Vishwanath Temple is one of the city's most prominent food landmarks, Kachori Gali. It is a street lined with black steaming kadais or cooking pots in which hot kachoris are prepared and served with chana and imli chutney. People arrive as early as 7 a.m. to beat the rush and taste the delicious snack.

Varanasi is home to many artisans who make brassware, copperware, glass bangles, wood, stone and clay toys. The city has an art centre that showcases and sells many local craft items.

The Ganga Arathi
The Ganga Arathi in Varanasi is a sight to behold. Young priests clad in saffron and cream sit on five raised platforms with an idol of the Goddess Ganga, a multi-tiered oil lamp, flowers, incense sticks, a conch shell, a brass lamp with a snake hood, and other brass pooja utensils. They synchronise a choreographed arathi procedure with orchestrated and pre-recorded chanting. Thousands of devotees visit the Dashashwamedh Ghat by foot and on boats to witness the arathi and the beauty of the hundreds of lamps that float in the Ganges.

Kal Bhairav Temple

Long ago, Lord Brahma proclaimed himself as the supreme being to the sages of the Sumeru Mountain. However, while consulting all four scriptures - the Rig, Yajur, Sam and Atharva Vedas, it was found that Lord Shiva was the ultimate being. After Brahma and Narayan laughed in disbelief, Shiva became furious and appeared as a stream of divine light amidst them. He created Kal Bhairav, the king of time, a ferocious avatar of himself. He is known as the policeman of Varanasi.

Many visit the Kal Bhairav temple to ward off the evil eye. Metal bracelets and black threads are sold outside the temple. Devotees believe that it gives them the protection of Kal Bhairav which guards them from negative energy that causes obstacles and hurdles in life.

Alamgiri Mosque

The Alamgiri Mosque was built in the 17th century by the Mughal king Aurangzeb and named after his honorific title ‘Alamgir’. It is also known as Beni Madhav ka Darera. Built over the ruins of a temple dedicated to Lord Vishnu in Varanasi, the mosque is a blend of Islamic and Hindu architecture. The mosque is situated on the Panchaganga Ghat where five streams converge.

Benares silk

Benares silk is so rooted in Indian culture that it has been cited in the Mahabharatha. There are four varieties of Benaresi silk – Katan or Pure Silk, Shattir, Organza and Georgette. There are over 10,000 shops in Varanasi that sell Benaresi silk saris. It is a cottage industry employing several thousand people in and around Varanasi. In the yesteryears, saris were made with real gold and silver zari and it could take nearly one year to finish a single sari.

Paan sellers of Benares

Paan is an after-meal delicacy made of betel leaves, betel nuts, and other ingredients. It enhances digestion and acts as a mouth freshener. Benaresi paan is very famous. There are over 15,000 paan stalls in Varanasi. The livelihood of around three to four lakh people in Varanasi depends on the paan business, which has a turnover of over two crore rupees every day. There are nearly 30 varieties of Benaresi paan and some can cost as much as 300 rupees.

Bulls and dogs of Benares

In Varanasi, bulls and dogs are considered sacred. Nandi, the bull is Lord Shiva's vahana (vehicle). He is considered a symbol of devotion and friendship. In every Shiva temple, one can find the idol of Nandi facing the deity. It is said that Nandi never leaves Shiva's side under any circumstance. He is portrayed as a great warrior in mythology. Dogs are the vahana of Kal Bhairav, an avatar of Lord Shiva. Feeding and taking care of dogs is considered a way of paying respect to the fierce deity who protects all the eight directions.

Kashi Vishwanath Temple

The word Kashi is derived from the Sanskrit word kas which means 'to shine'. It is believed that when the earth was created, the first ray of light fell on Kashi. The original temple was built in 1490 but was damaged repeatedly. Mughal king Aurangzeb destroyed the temple and built a mosque in its place. The temple was last built and restored to glory by the Queen of Indore, Rani Ahilya Bai Holkar. Some believe that the people of Varanasi hid the Shivalinga inside a well when they heard about Aurangzeb's plan to destroy the temple. The well is situated between the temple and the mosque and is worshipped by people even today.

Manikarnika Ghat

Manikarnika means 'earring' in Sanskrit. There are multiple stories attached to the significance of its name. Some people say Lord Shiva lost his earring while watching Lord Vishnu dig a pit with his Sudarshana Chakra. Another tale involves Goddess Parvathy lying to Lord Shiva about her lost earring in order to keep him from moving around with his devotees. It is said that every time a body is brought to the ghat for cremation, Shiva asks the soul if they have seen the manikarnika anywhere.

Some More Facts

The Bharat Mata temple has a huge marble map of India that covers today's India, Bangladesh and Pakistan. The map shows the mountains and terrains of India to-the-scale as per the geographical readings of the time.

The city has four main universities, Banaras Hindu University (BHU), Kashi Vidyapeeth, Sampoornand Sanskrit University and the Central University for Tibetan Studies. BHU is the largest university in Asia.

There is a special hostel in Varanasi where people check in to die. It is called the Mukthi Bhavan or Moksha Bhavan.

The city has countless temples devoted to Shaivism and Vaishnavism. It signifies harmony between both forms of Hinduism.

Varanasi has religious importance not only for Hindus, but also for Muslims, Jains and Buddhists.

Varanasi is also associated with the origin of Ayurveda and Yoga.

It is the birthplace of celebrated artists and scholars like acclaimed sitar player Ravi Shankar, and Tulsi Das who wrote the great epic Ramcharitmanas.

CHITRA SOUNDAR

Chitra hails from India, resides in London and lives in imaginary worlds weaved out of stories. She has written over twenty books for children aged 3 to 10 years. Chitra also loves to retell folktales, legends, and ancient tales from the Indian subcontinent. While she dabbles in chapter books, her first love is picture books.

SOUMITRA RANADE

Soumitra Ranade is an art director, illustrator, and filmmaker whose films have been screened internationally, including at Cannes. He works in the animation industry. He has written two books for children, both of which take inspiration from his sons' overactive imaginations.